Little Mitchie

LET'S LOOK INSIDE A TRAIN

LET'S LOOK INSIDE: VEHICLES

PAUL ZACHARY

CREATING YOUNG NONFICTION READERS

Little Mitchie books spark curiosity and support early nonfiction reading for students in Grades 2-3. Designed to build vocabulary, support second language learners, and prepare readers for middle-grade content, each book includes helpful tips for parents and educators to build confidence and deepen understanding of the world.

TIPS FOR READING NONFICTION WITH BEGINNING READERS

Talk about Nonfiction

Begin by explaining that nonfiction books give us information that is true. The book will be organized around a specific topic or idea, and we may learn new facts through reading.

Look at the Parts

Most nonfiction books have helpful features. Our *Little Mitchie* titles include color photographs and graphic aids, a table of contents, a glossary, and an index. Share the purpose of these features with your reader.

Color Photos and Graphic Aids

A lot of information can be found by "reading" photos, charts, maps, and other graphic aids found within nonfiction texts. Help your reader learn more about the different ways information can be displayed.

Table of Contents

Located at the front of the book, this list shows the big ideas within the text and the page numbers where they can be found.

Glossary

Located at the back of the book, the glossary defines key words and phrases that are related to the topic. These words and phrases can be found in the text in colored type.

Index

Located at the back of the book, an index is an alphabetical list of topics and the page numbers where they can be found.

With a little help and guidance about reading nonfiction, you can feel good about introducing a young reader to the world of *Little Mitchie* nonfiction books.

Little Mitchie is an imprint of:

Mitchell Lane
PUBLISHERS

2001 SW 31st Avenue
Hallandale, FL 33009
mitchelllanepub.com

First Edition, 2027.

Author: Paul Zachary
Designer: Rhea Magaro
Editor: Tricia Hoffman

Library of Congress Cataloging-in-Publication Data

Title: Let's Look Inside a Train / by Paul Zachary.

Description: Hallandale, FL :
Mitchell Lane Publishers, [2027]

Identifiers:
ISBN 979-8-89260-881-7 (library bound)
ISBN 979-8-90145-051-2 (paperback)
ISBN 979-8-89260-984-5 (eBook)

Library of Congress Control Number: 2026931209

Photo credits: Alamy: Dino Fracchia, 6; The Photo Works, 8; Shutterstock: aapsky cover, 1, 3, 4, 10, 17; fast-stock, 11; PICTOR PICTURES, 12; MaMbyM, 13; Jamie Fullerton UK, 14; ABB Photo, 16; Jacob Boomsma, 19; David Prado Perucha, 20; Locomotive74, 22

TABLE OF CONTENTS

Chapter One

THE JOURNEY BEGINS

All aboard! The **whistle** blows and the wheels of the long train begin to roll along the railroad tracks.

Have you ever wondered what it's like inside a train? Let's climb aboard and take a look!

TRAIN TIP

Some trains are more than one mile (1.6 kilometers) long. That's longer than 15 football fields!

TRAIN TIP

One locomotive can pull 100 or more train cars.

At the front of the train is the locomotive. There, the **engineer** sits in a tall blue seat. She is watching all the screens and shiny **controls**. She pulls a handle and the big engine rumbles like thunder.

Behind the locomotive is the baggage car, where suitcases and large travel bags are stored for the long ride.

Chapter Two

WINDOWS AND WARM MEALS

Next comes the **passenger coach**. Rows of seats are next to giant windows, and **luggage racks** stretch above the seats.

Passengers stretch their legs and get comfortable. They watch out the windows as houses, cars, and trees rush by.

Feeling hungry? For dinner, we go to the dining car. Many tables are covered with white tablecloths, shiny silverware, and sparkling dishes.

The chef cooks warm, delicious meals for everyone on board. Let's have lemon cake for dessert!

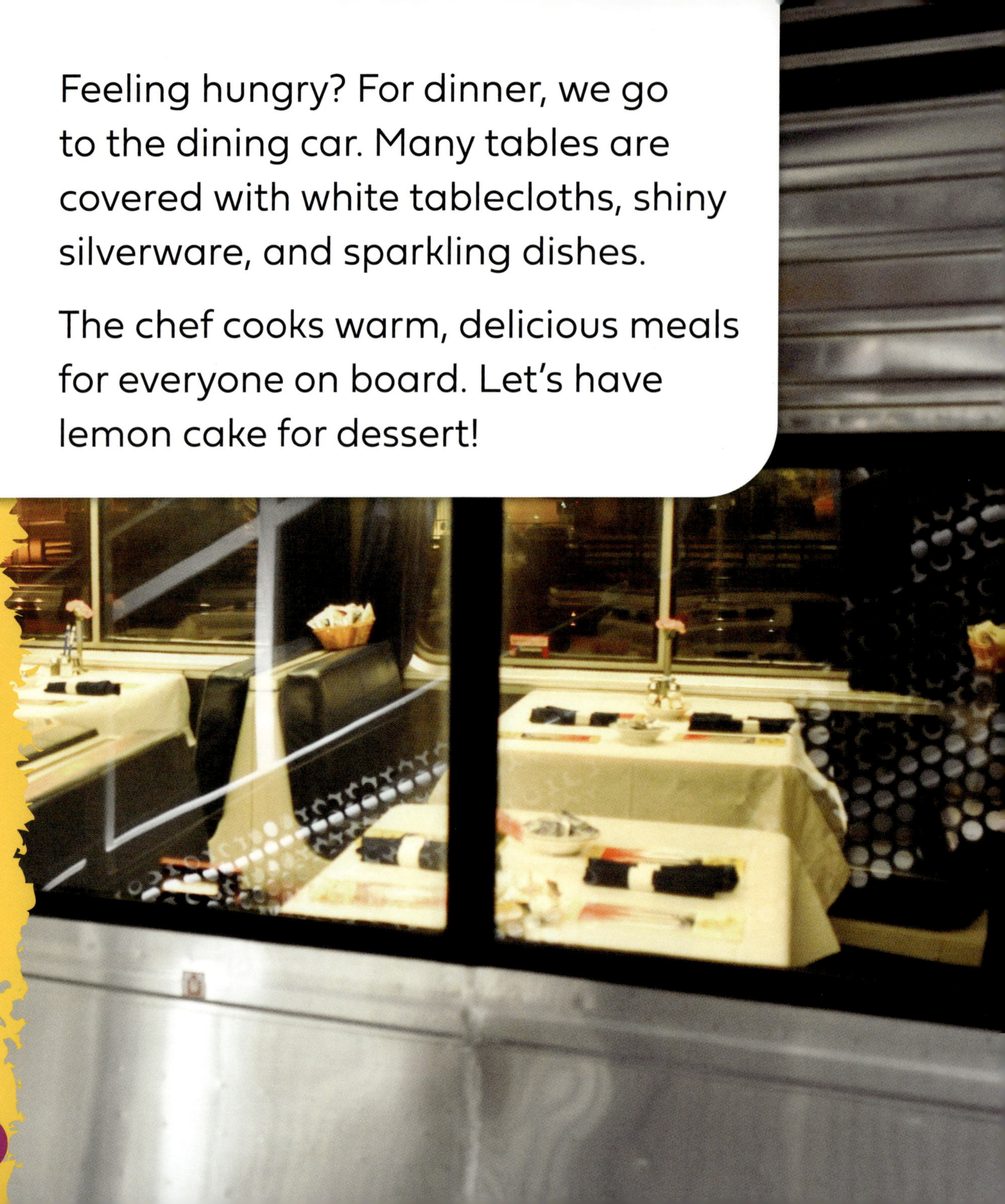

SALIDA DE EMERGENCIA
Templo Expiatorio

After dinner, we tiptoe into the quiet lounge car. Passengers relax in cozy chairs and on comfortable couches. Some read books. Others watch the scenery roll by as the train races through tunnels, over bridges, and across miles of rails.

TRAIN TIP

Sleeper cars were invented more than 150 years ago so passengers could rest during long trips.

Chapter Three

NIGHT ON THE RAILS

Farther back is the sleeper car. Rooms have tiny bunk beds with warm blankets and soft pillows for a good night's rest!

Tonight we will sleep on the train. Tomorrow we will wake up in a new city where many adventures await!

Chapter Four

A WORLD OF WONDERS

The last car is the **observation car**. Big windows let passengers have clear views of the beautiful scenery around them as mountains, rivers, and forests rush past.

The next time you hear a train whistle in the distance, wave hello. Inside every train is an adventure rolling down the tracks!

TRAIN TIP

Some trains run deep underground in tunnels below streets and buildings. These are called subways.

A LOOK INSIDE

GLOSSARY

coach (kohch) a train car where passengers sit and ride

controls (kuhn-trohlz) the levers, switches, and other devices used to operate a train

engineer (en-juh-neer) the person who drives and controls the train

locomotive (loh-kuh-moh-tiv) a train engine that pushes or pulls railroad cars

luggage rack (luhg-ij rak) a shelf above the seats where bags are stored

observation car (ahb-zur-vay-shuhn kahr) a train car with large windows for looking at the scenery

passenger (pas-uhn-jur) a person who rides in a vehicle such as a train, bus, or airplane

whistle (wis-uhl) a device that makes a loud sound to signal a train is coming

FURTHER READING

Pang, Ursula. *Trains.* PowerKids Press, 2025.

Rogers, Hal. *Trains.* The Child's World, 2024.

ON THE INTERNET

Train Facts
https://easyscienceforkids.com/all-about-trains/
Learn about the history of trains and see photos of the different types, such as steam trains, commuter trains, and high-speed trains.

California State Railroad Museum
www.californiarailroad.museum
Learn how trains work and see pictures of real locomotives and railroad cars.

INDEX